ACKNOWLEDGEMENT

I Would Like To Thank My Lord And Savior
Jesus Christ
For All That God Has Given Me
I Recognize That The Lord Gave Me This Gift
Which Allows Me To Share With Everyone That Participates In
The Reading Of The Literary Material That I Produce Through
The Commission Of God

Thank You Lord God
I Will Forever Be Grateful
For Your Trust In Me

Pamela Denise Brown

Anointed To Write

Color Me Is A Series Of Coloring Books That You Can Lose Yourself In And Relieve Stress…

SWAG – Men In Suits Is Therapeutic In That It Reduces Anxiety And Causes You To Focus And Relax…

SWAG – Men In Suits Is Filled With Pages To Color And Save, Along With Affirmations And Motivation That Motivates You To Take Action…

Coloring Books Are An In The Moment Activity And In Some Instances They Reduce Symptoms Of Depression And Help You To Concentrate…

Copyright © 2022

Pamela Denise Brown.
All rights reserved. No part of this book may be used or reproduced by any means, graphic, electronic, or mechanical, including photocopying, recording, taping or by any information storage retrieval system without the written permission of the publisher except in the case of brief quotations embodied in critical articles and reviews.

Pamela Denise Brown Books may be ordered through booksellers or by contacting:
Pamela Denise Brown Books.com
Or
Books Speak For You Publishing

The views expressed in this work are solely those of the author.
Any illustration provided by iStock and such images are being used for illustrative purposes.
Certain stock imagery © iStock.
ISBN: 978-1-64050-430-1

Printed in the United States Of America

40

Affirmations:

I Am A Great Leader

I Am Dependable

I Am Thoughtful

I Am Focused

I Am Making A Difference

I Am Dedicated To Being Better

I Am A Thought Leader

I Am Generous

I Am Caring

I Am Sincere

I Am Concerned

I Am Present

I Am Devoted To Making A Change In This World

I Am Respectful

I Am Smart

I Am Confident

I Am Successful

I Am Creative

I Am Organized

I Am Goal Oriented

I Am Loved…

Today

Today Is The Best Day Of My Life

Today Is A New Beginning For Me

Today I'm Taking Control Of My Life

Today I'm Going To Try Harder

Today I Won't Make Excuses

Today I Won't Complain

Today I Will Complete My Task

Today I Will Help Someone Else

Today Everything Changes For Me

Today I Become Responsible

Today I Won't Waste Another Minute

Today I Will Pursue My Dreams

Today I Will Challenge Myself

Today I Will Take Care Of Myself

Today I Become Stronger

Today I Will Start Pursing My Dreams

Today I Will Find Out How To Get What I Want Out Of Life

Today I Will Not Focus On Yesterday

Today I Will Try Harder Than I Tried Yesterday

Today I Will Realize That That Is A Gift...

Contact Information

pameladenisebrownbooks@yahoo.com

Publisher:

Website: Booksspeakforyou.com

A Little Information About The Author:

My Coloring Books, Inspirational Books, Motivational Journals And Healing Journals Are Designed To Guide Individuals To Becoming The Best Version Of There Selves…

My Reads Are Also Designed To Encourage, Enlighten, Strengthen And Cause People To Have A Closer Relationship With God…

I Write Children's Books To Help Children Become Psychologically Sociable, Culturally Sensitive And Aware So Children Can Co-Exist In Diversity And Become Successful At Life…

My Books Educate And Transform The Way People Think And Help People Develop And Grow Psychologically…

As An Ambassador For The Cultivation Of Children, I Am Inspiring Children To Think Differently…

I Present Adults And Children With An Opportunity To Replicate And Scale The Ideas From The Pages Of The Encouraging Literature I Produce Into Sustainable Change, With The Hopes Of Shaping The Lives Of People From Any Background, Community, Age, Ethnicity Or Gender…

My Goal Is To Give Adults And Children Balance And Direction And To Broaden Their Understanding Of Humanity As It Relates To "Co-Existing" In Society As A Coherent Whole…

The Messages In My Children's Books Subliminally Send The Same Message To Adults, Thereby Making Them Accountable To The Same Guidance…

Pamela Denise Brown

www.ingramcontent.com/pod-product-compliance
Lightning Source LLC
Chambersburg PA
CBHW080404170426
43193CB00016B/2802